A *terra magica* BOOK

HANNS REICH

LOVERS

HILL AND WANG · NEW YORK

Published in the United States of America by Hill and Wang, Inc.
Library of Congress catalog card number: 68–9301.
© 1968 Hanns Reich Verlag, Munich.
All rights reserved including diffusion by television.
Printed in Germany.

To his coy mistress

Had we but world enough, and time
This coyness, lady, were no crime.
We would sit down and think which way
To walk, and pass our long love's day;
Thou by the Indian Ganges' side
Shouldst rubies find; I by the tide
Of Humber would complain. I would
Love you ten years before the Flood;
And you should, if you please, refuse
Till the conversion of the Jews.
My vegetable love should grow
Vaster than empires, and more slow.
A hundred years should go to praise
Thine eyes, and on thy forehead gaze;
Two hundred to adore each breast,
But thirty thousand to the rest;
An age at least to every part,
And the last age should show your heart.
For, lady, you deserve this state,
Nor would I love at lower rate.

But at my back I always hear
Time's winged chariot hurrying near;
And yonder all before us lie
Deserts of vast eternity.
Thy beauty shall no more be found,
Nor in thy marble vault shall sound
My echoing song; then worms shall try
That long preserved virginity,
And your quaint honor turn to dust,
And into ashes all my lust.
The grave's a fine and private place,
But none, I think, do there embrace.

Now therefore, while the youthful hue
Sits on thy skin like morning dew,
And while thy willing soul transpires
At every pore with instant fires,
Now let us sport us while we may;
And now, like am'rous birds of prey,
Rather at once our time devour,
Than languish in his slow-chapped power.
Let us roll all our strength, and all
Our sweetness, up into one ball;

And tear our pleasures with rough strife
Through the iron gates of life.
Thus, though we cannot make our sun
Stand still, yet we will make him run.

Andrew Marvell (1621—1678)

To Celia

Kiss me, sweet: the weary lover
Can your favors keep, and cover,
When the common courting jay
All your bounties will betray.
Kiss again! no creature comes
Kiss, and score up wealthy sums
On my lips, thus hardly sundered,
While you breathe. First give a hundred,
Then a thousand, then another
Hundred, then unto the other
Add a thousand, and so more
Till you equal with the store
All the grass that Romney yields,
Or the sands in Chelsea fields,
Or the drops in silver Thames,
In the silent summer-nights,
When youths ply their stolen delights
That the curious may not know
How to tell 'em as they flow,
And the envious when they find
What their number is, be pined.

Gaius Valerius Catullus (84?—54 B.C.)
(translated by Ben Jonson, 1572—1637)

The song of songs, which is Solomon's

Let him kiss me with the kisses of his mouth; for thy
love is better than wine.

Because of the savor of thy good ointments thy name is
as ointment poured forth, therefore do the virgins love thee.

Draw me, we will run after thee: the King hath brought
me into his chambers: we will be glad and rejoice in thee,
we will remember thy love more than wine: the upright love thee

I am black but comely, O ye daughters of Jerusalem, as the
tents of Kedar, as the curtains of Solomon.

Look not upon me, because I am black, because the sun hath
looked upon me: my mother's children were angry with me;
they made me the keeper of the vineyards; but mine own vineyard
have I not kept.

Tell me, O thou whom my soul loveth, where thou feedest, where
thou makest thy flock to rest at noon: for why should I be as
one that turneth aside by the flocks of thy companions?

If thou know not, O thou fairest among women, go thy way forth
by the footsteps of the flock, and feed thy kids beside the
shepherds' tents.

I have compared thee, O my love, to a company of horses in
Pharaoh's chariots.

Thy cheeks are comely with rows of jewels, thy neck with
chains of gold.

We will make thee borders of gold with studs of silver.

While the King sitteth at his table, my spikenard sendeth
forth the smell thereof.

A bundle of myrrh is my well-beloved unto me; he shall lie
all night betwixt my breasts.

My beloved is unto me as a cluster of camphire in the vineyards
of Engedi.

Behold, thou art fair, my love; behold, thou art fair;
thou hast dove's eyes.

Behold, thou art fair, my beloved, yea, pleasant: also
our bed is green.

The beams of our house are cedar, and our rafters of fir.

I am the rose of Sharon, and the lily of the valleys.

As the lily among thorns, so is my love among the daughters.

As the apple tree among the trees of the wood, so is my beloved among the sons. I sat down under his shadow with great delight, and his fruit was sweet to my taste.

He brought me to the banqueting house, and his banner over me was love.

Stay me with flagons, comfort me with apples: for I am sick of love.

His left hand is under my head and his right hand doth embrace me.

I charge you, O ye daughters of Jerusalem, by the roes, and by the hinds of the field that ye stir not up, nor awake my love, till he please.

Canzone: Of the gentle heart

Within the gentle heart Love shelters him
As birds within the green shade of the grove.
Before the gentle heart, in Nature's scheme,
Love was not, nor the gentle heart ere Love.
For with the sun, at once,
So sprang the light immediately; nor was
Its birth before the sun's.
And Love hath his effect in gentleness
Of very self; even as
Within the middle fire the heat's excess.

Guido Guinicelli (1240?—1274)
(translated by Dante Gabriel Rossetti, 1828—1882)

Sonnets from the Portuguese

XIV

If thou must love me, let it be for nought
Except for love's sake only. Do not say
"I love her for her smile—her look—her way
Of speaking gently,—for a trick of thought
That falls in well with mine, and certes brought
A sense of pleasant ease on such a day"—
For these things in themselves, Beloved, may
Be changed, or change for thee,—and love, so wrought,
May be unwrought so. Neither love me for
Thine own dear pity's wiping my cheeks dry,—
A creature might forget to weep, who bore
Thy comfort long, and lose thy love thereby!
But love me for love's sake, that evermore
Thou may'st love on, through love's eternity.

Elizabeth Barrett Browning (1806—1861)

Sonnet XXXIII

Full many a glorious morning have I seen
Flatter the mountain-tops with sovereign eye,
Kissing with golden face the meadows green,
Gilding pale streams with heavenly alchemy;
Anon permit the basest clouds to ride
With ugly rack on his celestial face,
And from the forlorn world his visage hide,
Stealing unseen to west with this disgrace.
Even so my sun one early morn did shine
With all-triumphant splendor on my brow;
But out, alack! he was but one hour mine;
The region cloud hath masked him from me now.
   Yet him for this my love no whit disdaineth;
   Suns of the world may stain when heaven's sun staineth.

William Shakespeare (1564—1616)

from Aucassin and Nicolette

Who would list to the good lay
Gladness of the captive gray?
'Tis how two young lovers met,
Aucassin and Nicolette,
Of the pains the lover bore
And the sorrows he outwore,
For the goodness and the grace,
Of his love, so fair of face.

Sweet the song, the story sweet,
There is no man hearkens it,
No man living 'neath the sun,
So outwearied, so foredone,
Sick and woeful, worn and sad,
But is healed, but is glad,
   'Tis so sweet.

The "Old Captive" (1130?)
(translated by Andrew Lang, 1844—1912)

from Astrophel and Stella

Because I breathe not love to every one,
  Nor do not use set colors for to wear,
  Nor nourish special locks of vowed hair,
  Nor give each speech a full point of a groan,
The courtly nymphs, acquainted with the moan
  Of them who in their lips Love's standard bear,
  "What, he!" say they of me, "Now I dare swear
  He cannot love; no, no, let him alone.
And think so still, so Stella know my mind;
  Profess indeed I do not Cupid's art;
  But you, fair maids, at length this true shall find,
That his right badge is but worn in the heart;
  Dumb swans, not chatt'ring pies, do lovers prove;
  They love indeed who quake to say they love,.

Sir Philip Sidney (1554—1586)

Mother, I cannot wind my wheel

Mother, I cannot wind my wheel;
  My fingers ache, my lips are dry;
Oh! if you felt the pain I feel!
  But oh, who ever felt as I!

Sappho (about 610 B.C.)
(translated by Walter Savage Landor, 1775—1864)

What is most to be liked in a mistress

'Tis not how witty nor how free
Nor yet how beautiful she be,
But how much kind and true to me.
Freedom and wit none can confine,
And beauty like the sun doth shine,
But kind and true are only thine.

Let others with attention sit,
To listen, and admire her wit;
That is a rock where I ne'er split.
Let others dote upon her eyes,
And burn their hearts for sacrifice,
Beauty's a calm where danger lies.

Yet kind and true have long been tried,
A harbor where we may confide
And safely there at anchor ride.
From change of winds there we are free,
Nor need we fear storm's tyranny,
Nor pirate, though a prince he be.

Aurelian Townshend (1583—1651?)

John Anderson my jo

John Anderson my jo, John,
When we were first acquent,
Your locks were like the raven,
Your bonnie brow was brent
But now your brow is beld, John,
Your looks are like the snow,
But blessings on your frosty pow,
John Anderson, my jo!

John Anderson my jo, John,
We clamb the hill thegither,
And monie a cantie day, John,
We've had wi' ane anither:
Now we maun totter down, John,
And hand in hand we'll go,
And sleep thegither at the foot,
John Anderson, my jo!

Robert Burns (1759—1796)

The song of Troylus

If no love is, O God, what fele I so?
And if love is, what thinge and whiche is he?
If love be gode, from whennes cometh my wo?
If it be wykke, a wonder thynketh me,
When every torment and adversite,
That cometh of him, may to me savory thynke
For ay thirst I the more that Iche it drynke.

   And if that in myn owne lust I brenne,
From whennes cometh my wailynge and my pleynte?
If harme agree me, whereto pleyne I thenne?
I noot, ne why, unwery, that I feynte.
O quyke deth! O swete harm so queynte!
How may I se in me swiche quantite,
But if that I consente that it so be?

   And if that I consente, I wrongfully
Compleyne ywis; thus possed to and fro,
Al sterelees withinne a boot am I
Amyd the see, betwexen windes two,
That in contrarie standen ever mo.
Allas! what is this wonder maladye?
For hete of cold, for cold of hete I dye.

Francesco Petrarca (1304—1374)
(translated by Geoffrey Chaucer, 1340—1400)

Photographers

Front cover: Weisweiler-Collignon
 1   Astrid von Luttitz
 2   Wolfgang Etzold-Anthony
 3   Robert Häusser
 4   Hanns Reich
 5   Hans Steiner-Collignon
 6   Jochen Blume
 7   Dr. Othmar Herbst-Anthony
 8   Joachim Schultz
 9   Reiner Ruthenbeck
10   Ralf Döring
11   Barbara Niggl
12   Georg Oddner
13   Gert Kreutschmann
14   Will McBride
15   Collignon
16   Oscar van Alphen
17   Guido Mangold
18   Thomas Höpker-Pontis
19   Stefan Moses
20   Hilmar Pabel
21   Thomas Höpker-Pontis
22   Armin Haab
23   René Burri-Magnum
25   Werner Koblizek
26   Gotthard Schuh
27   Thomas Höpker
28   Barbara Niggl-Pontis
29   Horst Munzig
30   Wolfgang Haut
31   Anders Holmquist – twen
32   Thomas Höpker
33   Li Erben-Bittins
34   Roman W. Kochalski-Bavaria
35   Thomas Höpker
36   Will McBride
37   Will McBride
38   Rudolf Dietrich
39   Thomas Höpker
40   Hilmar Pabel
41   Lucien Le Chevillier
42   Bernd Kortner
43   Evelin Menzel
44   Horst Munzig
45   Stefan Moses
46   Hanns Hubmann
47   Daniela Sýkorová
48   Oscar van Alphen
49   Georg Oddner
50   Wolfgang Haut
51   Rudolf Dietrich
52   Gerhard Hanig
53   Lawrence Le Guay
54   Jean Louis Swiners
55   Will McBride
56   Ilse Mayer-Gehrken
57   Piet Blaak
58   Robert Häusser
59   Ernst Harstrick-Mauritius
60   Gunther Radloff
61   Günther Hoffmann
62   Fernand Rausser
63   Paul Almasy
64   René Maltête
Back cover: Bruno Mooser

34

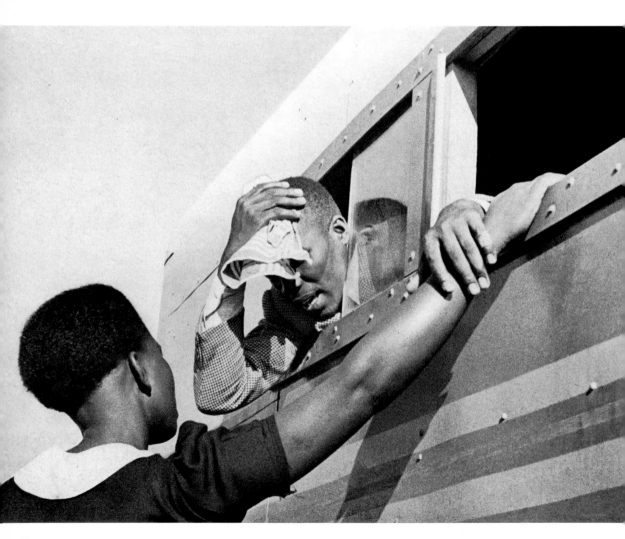

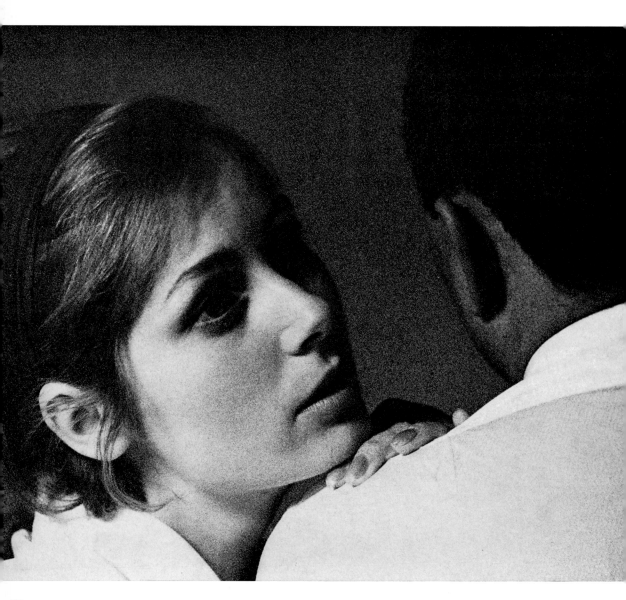

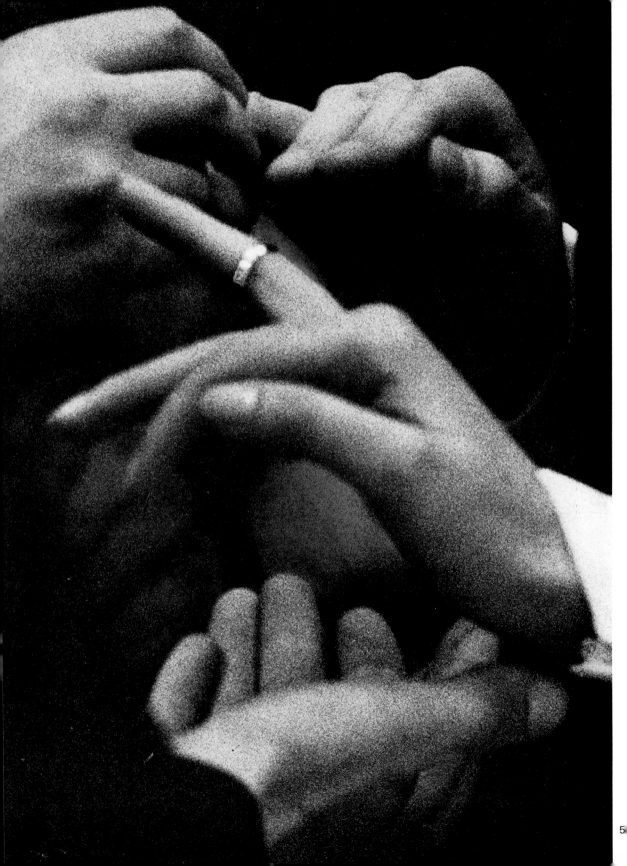

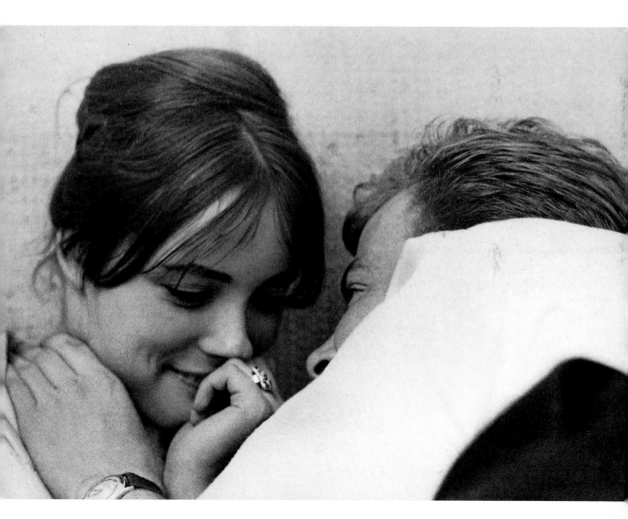